Indian Weddings

Photo by Dallan Photography
Omna and Koushik Bhattacharya married on August 30, 2008,
at the Landsdowne Resort in Virginia.

Indian Weddings

Simran Chawla

Schiffer Publishing Ltd

4880 Lower Valley Road, Atglen, PA 19310

Other Schiffer Books on Related Subjects:

Bridal Flowers: Bouquets, Boutonnièrs, Corsages, 978-0-7643-3485-6, $24.99

Before You Buy an Engagement Ring, 978-0-7643-0611-1, $12.95

Accessorizing the Bride: Vintage Wedding Finery through the Decades, 978-0-7643-2185-4, $49.95

"Symbol of Happiness" © Yuliya Konyayeva. Image from BigStockPhoto.com.
"Patterned Elephants" © Yuliya Konyayeva. Image from BigStockPhoto.com.
"Henna Mandala" © Krishna Somya. Image from BigStockPhoto.com.
"Handmade" © Asmaa Murad. Image from BigStockPhoto.com.
"Handmade" © Asmaa Murad. Image from BigStockPhoto.com.
"Background13" © Jennifer Westmoreland. Image from BigStockPhoto.com.
"Paisley Flower Texture Design" © Yih Graphic. Image from BigStockPhoto.com.
"Book" © Zhen Guo. Image from BigStockPhoto.com.
"Abstract Background" © Andrew Khritin. Image from BigStockPhoto.com.

Designed by John P. Cheek
Type set in Zapfino Forte LT Pro/Minion Pro/Gill Sans MT Pro

ISBN: 978-0-7643-3547-1

Printed in China

Schiffer Books are available at special discounts for bulk purchases for sales promotions or premiums. Special editions, including personalized covers, corporate imprints, and excerpts can be created in large quantities for special needs. For more information contact the publisher:

Published by Schiffer Publishing Ltd.
4880 Lower Valley Road
Atglen, PA 19310
Phone: (610) 593-1777; Fax: (610) 593-2002
E-mail: Info@schifferbooks.com

For the largest selection of fine reference books on this and related subjects, please visit our website at
www.schifferbooks.com
We are always looking for people to write books on new and related subjects. If you have an idea for a book please contact us at the above address.

This book may be purchased from the publisher.
Include $5.00 for shipping.
Please try your bookstore first.
You may write for a free catalog.

In Europe, Schiffer books are distributed by
Bushwood Books
6 Marksbury Ave.
Kew Gardens
Surrey TW9 4JF England
Phone: 44 (0) 20 8392 8585; Fax: 44 (0) 20 8392 9876
E-mail: info@bushwoodbooks.co.uk
Website: www.bushwoodbooks.co.uk

To my parents, who have given me endless love.

With all my heart, I say thanks...

I seem to have loved you in numberless forms, numberless times,
In life after life, in age after age forever.

–Rabindranath Tagore

Omna and Koushik Bhattacharya, married on August 30, 2008, at the Landsdowne Resort in Virginia.

Contents

Photo by CB ART PHOTOGRAPHY / Chandrakant Patel

Preface

Congratulations on your upcoming wedding!
Cheers to a future of shared happiness, love and companionship.

Oh, love. We all crave it. And if you've grown up on a steady diet of retro Bollywood as I have, you're likely a love junky, addicted to the promise of undying romance and happy endings. You grow to expect love, to wait for it, to ache for it, and to suddenly be consumed by it when it truly finds you. But once you embrace the sheer life changing force of it and adjust to its reality, here's hoping you and yours fall into a partnership of equality and balance, of lifelong love and companionship.

It's my hope that this book may help you create a meaningful experience as you express your love and celebrate your commitment. Whether including elements of South Asian culture in your wedding is a matter of tradition or trend, heritage or habit, I hope you will find inspiration in these pages. The many cultures of the vast subcontinent are as diverse as they are complex, and the traditions Indian Americans have adopted are similarly extensive. While I hoped to showcase a range of Indian American customs across faiths and cultures from recent weddings across the country, I know that much is missing from this brief collection. I hope you will look to your family and soon-to-be-family as your number one resource to question and gain further understanding of the rituals and the culture that has defined so many of our lives.

The eternal strength of Indian culture has kept its social customs and religious practices in tact for centuries and today binds scattered children of immigrants to each another and to a vitality thousands of miles away. Through the framework of an Indian wedding *outside of India*, that connection is magnified, as a Punjabi wedding will likely follow a similar sequence of customs whether it's hosted in Nairobi or Sydney, London or Toronto. Though trend may vary, core traditions are similar. For all its flaws and all its strengths, an Indian wedding is a powerhouse of culture, and under the superficial, sensory draw of colorful chaos lies the essence of Indian American life. As they follow the footsteps of tradition, Indian American couples across the country are marking their impressions on an inherited culture. Admittedly, having an Indian wedding for some is a burden of obedience, and for others Indian weddings are merely a matter of trend. So, I question if the strength of Indian culture will last in America. I question if the great-grandchildren of Indian immigrants will have the same wedding experiences of my generation, one that has been so guided by our parents and our direct links to India. As one of many children of Indian immigrants, I hope this book may serve as a snapshot of Indian American wedding celebrations today.

Acknowledgments

To the talented photographers who didn't hesitate to share with me their creative visions, I sincerely thank you for your joyful art. Your photographs are truly inspiring. To the brides and grooms who shared with me their personal stories of family tradition and ceremony, I thank you for letting me relive your special day. And a most heartfelt thank you to my brother Teji, sister-in-law Aman, and my dearest friends who talked me through this project every single day. Your encouragement has driven me to complete this most special project, my first book.

Introduction
Married in America

My parents were not the arranged marriage types.
Unlike the rush of immigrant couples they joined when they moved from India in the mid 1970s, my parents were unmarried when they landed in this country. They hadn't even met. Busy working odd jobs and making New York City home, it was months before they were introduced. After a casual courtship easing into love over shared slices of pizza near Rockefeller Center and developing a friendship in those early, homesick days, they decided to get married.

The wedding took place in the unlikely town of Charleston, West Virginia, where a handful of my dad's family lived and a small Indian community was settling in. There was no Sikh temple in Charleston so family stepped in to create a makeshift temple in my uncle's living room. My dad's eldest brother in the States officiated a Sikh ceremony, and his sisters cooked a celebratory dinner for a house packed with kids, family members, and nearby friends. My mom didn't have any family in the country. Her sister sent a package from India—a hand embroidered gold and red sequined bridal sari along with blessings lettered on light blue sheets of Air Mail. The wedding was the best they could do to respect Punjabi wedding customs in a country that still seemed so foreign.

But that was thirty years ago.

Fast forward to my brother's recent wedding where he arrived to his ceremony at a gated Sikh temple on horseback with a bus load of family and friends dancing to a *dholi's* beats behind him. Hundreds of guests attended the morning ceremony and a glittering evening reception at a manor estate where Indian food and music topped the night. This is the new norm for Indian American weddings.

Since the time of my parents' wedding, the Indian community has established firm roots in America. Though we've established a place for ourselves in mainstream American society, million dollar temples and over-stocked Indian grocery stores offer tangible connections to a culture thousands of miles away. But nowhere is that connection more visualized and more celebrated than in Indian American weddings.

I hear it all the time: *Indians are obsessed with weddings.* Often days long and massive in size, today's Indian wedding events fill grand hotel ballrooms to capacity where food, dress, henna, jewelry, music, and ceremony strive to be as authentic as a wedding in India and more glitzy than a Bollywood blockbuster. In a culture so defined by relationships, Indian weddings pay tribute to one of the most important relationships in a person's lifetime. But I wonder, by following traditional Indian wedding customs, what is it exactly that we as Indian Americans are trying to recreate? Are our weddings an over-the-top attempt to connect to our parents' heritage or an honest reflection of how we were raised? Are they a display of wealth and status or a celebration of culture? In trying to follow Indian customs, have we created our own wedding traditions, fulfilling the customs that best fit into American life? What do our weddings say about us? And most importantly, what do you want your wedding to say about you?

Today's spectacularly grand weddings seem to be a relatively recent phenomenon of the last decade or two, as families are more likely to spend their amassed wealth, and as Indian resources have become more available in America, an Indian wedding industry has taken shape.

When Mini and Montu Chatterjee got married sixteen years ago, they pulled off what seems to be impossible these days. They planned a wedding in just two weeks.

"Weddings weren't so elaborate those days, or didn't seem to be," said Mini who lives with her husband and two daughters in Maryland. Her wedding was a simple affair in her childhood home in Olney. To create the basics of a Hindu wedding, her mother Mona took charge. She hired local carpenters to construct a *mandap*, an altar, and a *doli*, a ceremonial carriage in which the bride's brothers carry her after the ceremony. Mona hand painted the wooden framework of both pieces gold and red and around the mandap she hung garlands of flowers. She draped the doli with fabric and filled it with satin cushions that she had sewn and beaded herself.

"I still have the doli," said Mini. "I've thought about giving it away, but it has such sentimental value for me," she said.

Certainly, today's bride doesn't need to build a doli from scratch. She can rent one online, from a local Indian store or from wedding decorators like Prabha Bhambri, of Virginia.

Prabha's home feels like a treasure chest, loaded with mixed sizes of bronze and porcelain statues of Hindu deities like Ganesha, Laxmi, and Hanuman. Peacock feathers sit next to starched golden turbans, tall candles, color palettes, and beaded fabric swatches—all pieces that play a part in her elaborate designs. But if her house is a treasure chest, her Maryland warehouse is the coveted vault, packed with

mandaps, dolis, and larger pieces that were custom built for couples.

"Every wedding is different. Indian brides now are more confident, more selective than in the past. They don't just follow old traditions, they believe in their own ideas and have creative visions of what they want," said Prabha, who moved to the country 40 years ago.

Prabha has worked in this business for over a decade now and has watched as wedding trends have evolved. Where customary reds and golds were the consistent color schemes of weddings in the past, now Tiffany Blues, hot pink palettes, and peacock mélanges—striking blues, deep emerald greens, and purple hues—are the latest demand.

But in the end, it's not about trends, said Prabha. "It's about joining two families." To her clients, she often suggests adding symbolic gestures to the wedding events that are not distinctly "Indian" touches, like a mother-daughter dance or joint lighting of candles by the bride and groom's family.

"It's time to start new traditions," she said.

At the heart of it all, under the weighted layers of color and custom, whether the essence of Indian weddings reflects tradition or trend, there's no doubt that today's ceremonies pay tribute to family and illuminate a cultural respect for relationships. Families come together because everyone has a role to play, whether it's the sister of the groom or the brother of the bride's mother. Weddings are the new family reunion. While they are a celebration of sacred commitment, joining two lives and merging two families, they are also a time to reunite, bringing relatives that are scattered all over the world to come together again as a family.

Photo by Dallan Photography

Words of Wisdom

We decided to have an Indian-style wedding because…

"Although we grew up in America, we wanted to experience the rich traditions of our Indian heritage."

–Omna Kohli, August 30, 2008, Lansdowne, Virginia

"It's our culture and there was no question it would be an Indian-themed wedding."

–Eena Sidhu, June 27, 2009, Waldorf, Maryland

"We wanted to get married in the most traditional way possible and also because we felt that Indian weddings have the most beautiful traditions and decorations. The majority of our guests were Indian so we knew they would appreciate it."

–Chinar Desai, August 22, 2009, Springfield, PA

"It was important to our families and we felt the traditional Indian Christian service held a lot of meaning and rich heritage."

–Bincy Puthenmadathi, August 11, 2007, Randolph, NJ

"Never in my wildest dreams did I think it'd be Indian style but my husband is Indian and it was in his blood to do it this way."

–Jenny Ahuja, Sikh ceremony and reception, November 26, 2006, Baltimore, MD, and Catholic wedding and reception, December 2, 2006, Miami, FL

"… of the rich colors, our heritage, the traditions, the uniqueness we have in our culture, and of all the celebrator moments we share with everyone."

–Poonam Rakkar, April 11, 2009, Modesto, California

"Our culture is very important to us (both of us are Indian); so it was a no-brainer."

–Meghana Acharya, June 6, 2009, San Ramon, CA

"I'm Indian and it's the only type of wedding I grew up dreaming about."

–Rupa Gill, May 16, 2004, Charleston, WV

"I felt it was important to cherish the rich culture and heritage we belong too, and although I didn't understand each ritual in detail, I understood that the importance of family and togetherness was a key foundation to our traditional Sikh weddings."

–Simi Grewal-Singh, February 10, 2007, Fremont, CA

"Our culture is a big part of our roots, upbringing, and our everyday lives. It was important to us to incorporate both aspects of our Indian and American background into a culturally infused celebration. Although it was very difficult and time consuming, it all paid off in the end."

–Nazia Khan, July 18, 2008, Chicago, IL

"We are proud of our culture and we wanted our guests to embrace the Indian culture and how magical and special it is, especially being children who were born and raised in the US."

–Kajal Patel, Saturday June 27, 2009, Cherry Hill, NJ

"I think it's visually and spiritually one of the most beautiful cultures in the world and being born and raised Indian, we wouldn't have it any other way."

–Ameeta Singh, June 3, 2006, Fairfax, VA

"Indian culture is one of the most colorful, festive, and romantic cultures, which served as perfect backdrop for us to express our emotions on how we were feeling on the inside."

–Navleen Sandhu, October 29, 2005, Gaithersburg, MD

"As non traditional as we are, our wedding day was something that we both wanted to be traditional but on our own terms."

–Tanisha Gulhar, May 24, 2008, Reston Town Center, VA

Section 1: Planning Basics

Photo by Milton Yin
Don't let the stress of wedding planning get the best of you.

Getting Started

As weddings continue to grow in scale and drama across America, planning *and surviving* a wedding is likely the first major obstacle in a couple's shared journey. The demands of decision-making and the stress of managing logistics, ballooning budgets, and family expectations can stifle the most enthusiastic of couples, especially for Indian American weddings that include multiple events. But it's not all doom and gloom. You might be surprised at how much you learn about yourself and your capacities to compromise, lead, and love as a couple in those months before your wedding. And remember, at the end of the day, good people throw a good party.

With more and more resources available, planning an Indian wedding is a daunting challenge if you don't make some big decisions right at the start. Here are some general, big picture thoughts to consider when you first begin to plan your wedding:

Wish List: Communicate expectations early on. What's on your wedding wish list? What are both families' visions of this wedding? With bridal showers, bachelorette parties, engagement parties, mehndi nights, sangeets, farewell lunches, not to mention the wedding ceremony, and customs that lead up to it topped off by a reception... how much is too much for you? Decide what elements are really important to you, and what you wouldn't mind skipping out on. As a couple, work with both families and discuss a wedding that reflects your personality and style, as well as your traditions.

It Takes a Village: From henna artists to florists, mandap designers to dhol players, it truly takes a village of vendors to contribute to your big day. Browse an endless selection of vendors online, but old-fashioned word-of-mouth recommendations can be priceless. When you attend a wedding, pay attention to details that take your fancy. Did you like the bride's makeup? Follow up and ask her about her makeup artist's services. Look for vendors with a solid reputation and ask to contact some of their previous clients. When you decide on a vendor, always ask for a contract. Working with vendors from the South Asian community can sometimes be informal, like asking for a favor from family. But contracts are critical to protect your investments. Develop a good working relationship with your vendors so you can trust them on your big day.

Let's Be Realistic: Calculate a *realistic* budget and plan within its framework. Some can, but most people can't have it all, so pick your priorities and adjust your budget. Is it more important to spend a hefty sum on entertainment or on photography? On a dramatic *baraat* or on a one-of-a-kind cake? Budgets are driven by guest count, so be mindful of your capacities. On the flip side, be realistic about what you *can* afford. Most vendors are open to negotiate their fees slightly, but don't expect to set your own rates for every service. (See page 21 for a complete budget checklist.)

Synchronize Your Watches: It doesn't have to be the most chaotic day of your life. Avoid confusion and stress by making a comprehensive timeline and sticking to it. What time will you wake up? What time will you leave the house? What time will the caterer arrive? And the decorator? With so many moving parts, it's vital to get your vendors, family, and friends on the same timeline so the key players know where to be and what to expect on the wedding day. One delay will cause another, so avoid a domino effect and stay on schedule.

That Special Someone: You've already found that special someone, now help your vendors find that one contact person who they can rely on throughout the wedding. This contact—a close friend or family member—can assist the wedding planner and photographer to decipher who's who during the events, and can keep communication flowing if language is an issue.

Play Up Your Personality: Indian weddings are certainly family events, but as a couple, how can you bring your personalities into it? Every element of your wedding can have a personal touch, from the stationary to the music to the menus. When it comes to food, it's easy to feel "*desi* overload" with so many back-to-back events, so mix up the palette and offer varied tastes for different events—think about bringing in your favorite non-Indian flavors or cocktails.

Your Day, Your Way: Don't be afraid to ask for what you want. If you reach out to vendors or venues that aren't familiar with South Asian weddings, don't assume that they can't provide what you'll need. More often than not, if you explain in detail what you want, they can make it happen.

Your Traditions: Take the time to learn about your family traditions. You're investing so much time and money in this wedding… don't fake it. Research, question, and understand the rituals that are about to change your life. Your family is your best resource.

Photo Courtesy Engaging Affairs
For Neil and Shilpi Agarwal's reception, the cocktail hours had a contemporary, lounge-feel, with a sleek black and white palette accentuated with reds.

Photo Courtesy Engaging Affairs
For the reception, the couple opted for a more traditional mix of reds, purples, and gold. "Nothing is standard anymore, it's all about what's important to you," says Sara Muchnik of Engaging Affairs.

CB Art Photography/Chandrakant Patel

Don't forget to budget wedding day transportation for the bride and groom. Neha and Anurag Chhabra cruised through their day in a white Rolls Royce.

Photo by Yogi Patel of Global Photography L.A.

Photo by Yogi Patel of Global Photography L.A.

Some Cost Cutting Tips
• Inquire about hidden fees, like corkage fees, cake cutting fees, etc.
• Consider hosting Friday or Sunday events instead of Saturday, when costs are at their peak.
• Avoid hosting events near holidays like Valentine's Day or Mother's Day, when flowers are more expensive.
• Browse Craigslist.com and other online sources for bargains and vendors looking to get started in the business.
• Keep track of your head count. As your guest list expands, so do your costs.

Budget Checklist ✔

Use this checklist as a preliminary base to start calculating your budget.

It's helpful to break up your budget by event, though many vendors can offer bundle packages if they provide services for multiple events. For most of your events, you'll need to consider these costs:

	Estimate	Actual
Main Expenses		
Venue Fees	$	$
Rental Fees (tables, chairs, and extras)	$	$
Food and Service	$	$
Beverages	$	$
Decorations (mandap, stages, centerpieces, lighting, flowers, etc.)	$	$
Music (DJ or live performers)	$	$
Officiant Fee or Temple Donation	$	$
Guest Favors	$	$
Accessories (flower garlands, extras, etc.)	$	$
Cake	$	$
Stationary		
Invitations	$	$
Accessories (save the date, programs, menu cards, place cards, & thank you cards)	$	$
Postage	$	$
Baraat (the groom's procession)		
Groom's Transportation (horse, elephant, or car)	$	$
NOTE: You may need to pay for a permit for a horse or elephant baraat.		
Music (dhol player, live band, or DJ)	$	$
Groom's Family Transportation	$	$
Attire		
Bride & Groom:		
Wedding ceremony attire	$	$
Wedding ceremony jewelry	$	$
Wedding attire accessories	$	$
Reception attire	$	$
Reception jewelry	$	$
Reception attire accessories	$	$
Pre-wedding events attire and jewelry	$	$
Bride:		
Hair and makeup	$	$
Henna	$	$

	Estimate	Actual
Bridal Party:		
Hair and makeup	$	$
Henna	$	$
Photography		
Photography Package	$	$
Videography Package	$	$
Rings		
Bride's Ring	$	$
Groom's Ring	$	$
Gifts		
Bride's Family to Groom's Family	$	$
Groom's Family to Bride's Family	$	$
Transportation		
Bride & Groom: Wedding day	$	$
Transportation for Out-of-Town Guests	$	$
Valet Parking	$	$
Trip to India (or elsewhere)		
Flights	$	$
Visas	$	$
Domestic Travel in Country	$	$
Gifts to Family	$	$
Hotel	$	$
Food	$	$
Shopping List	$	$
Honeymoon		
Flights	$	$
Visas	$	$
Hotel	$	$
Food and Drink	$	$
Miscellaneous	$	$
Totals:	$	$

Photo by CB ART PHOTOGRAPHY / Chandrakant Patel

Planning Schedule

Of course, a wedding is about the bride and groom. But truly, your wedding also honors your culture, your families, your new relationships, and the traditions both families hope to keep alive through you. As you begin your wedding planning process, consider these suggestions.

At Least a Year in Advance
Discuss, discuss, discuss…

- Introduce both immediate families.
- Decide in which city the wedding events will take place.
- Discuss which events will happen on the bride's side, on the groom's side, and which events will be jointly hosted.
- Come up with a preliminary budget and sort out who pays for what. This can be dicey, but needs to happen early. The days of the bride's family paying for everything are no longer. These days, typically, both families split the cost of the wedding weekend.
- Discuss expectations of the events with both sets of parents. Big or small scale? Traditional or mix of cultures? What does each tradition mean to each family? Which traditions would you and your fiancé rather skip?
- Discuss the wedding date. Who chooses the date? Will a *pandit,* or priest, be consulted?
- Begin researching venues.

Photo by Robert Isacson
Blending his Indian and her Lebanese traditions, Kavi and Maria's wedding honored both of their cultures. The couple cut the cake with a Lebanese ceremonial sword. It's never too early to discuss which wedding traditions matter to you.

Eight Months in Advance
Research and be inspired…

- Finalize a wedding date
- Scout venues for all of your events. Book them as soon as you can.
- If your ceremony will not be in a temple, book your religious officiant.
- Research and meet with vendors like caterers, photographers, decorators, DJs, videographers, mehndi artists, dhol players, baraat transportation (horse, car, etc), hair and makeup artists, and seamstress.
- Agree to a first draft guest list.
- If you plan to go abroad for wedding shopping, book your trip.

Six Months in Advance
Book it!

- Send out Save the Date cards to family and friends that will definitely be invited.
- Finalize and sign contracts with your vendors
- Select your wedding party of bridesmaids and groomsmen (if you choose to have attendants).
- Decide on wedding day attire for the bride, groom, family members, and those in your wedding party.
- Order your wedding cake.
- Scout locations to house out-of-town guests and reserve a block of rooms.

Photo by Yogi Patel of Global Photography L.A.
For a picture perfect venue like Neha and Anurag's wedding on Huntington Beach, CA, it's smart to scout and book venues almost a year in advance.

- Book your honeymoon. Check your passport, obtain visas, and find out what vaccines you'll need if you're going abroad.
- Begin beauty and fitness regimens if you have specific goals.
- Choose items for your bridal registry.
- Decide on décor for the events—discuss details like lighting, mandaps, etc.
- Schedule hair and makeup appointments
- Start actively gathering addresses for those on your guest list.
- Set a date to get a marriage license (check with your state government for details on marriage licenses).
- Create a wedding website to update your family and friends and indicate where people can upload their photos after the wedding.
- Order wedding invitations. Set the RSVP date for four weeks before the wedding.

Three Months in Advance
It's all about the details…

- Book transportation arrangements for out-of-town guests and wedding day transportation for the bride and groom.
- Finalize guest list.
- If you're going abroad for wedding shopping, now's the time to go. It can take several weeks to custom tailor a bridal outfit, so you want to leave yourself enough time.
- Decide what performances or speeches (if any) you want during your events. Reach out to your friends and family and give them time to plan their performances.
- Arrange favors to be given out at your various events.
- Finalize wedding day attire and accessories for bride, groom, and families.
- Determine gifts that will be given to the "other side" (gifts from the bride's family to the groom's family and vice versa).
- Meet with your stylist for a trial hair and makeup run-through.
- Confirm that you and your fiancé understand the rituals of your ceremonies

Two Months in Advance
Make the pieces fit…

- Send out your invitations.
- Make song selections—what song will play as you're introduced for the first time? When you cut the cake? Your first dance? What songs *don't* you want played?
- Determine a final itinerary for each of your events.
- Make sure everyone understands their responsibilities if they play a role in any of your events.
- Discuss the events and etiquette with any guests that aren't familiar with your traditions.
- Meet with your photographer at the various venues. Run through the different ceremonies if he/she is not familiar with your traditions.

Photo by Glenn Barnett
You've tasted it, you've ordered it. Now think about when you'll cut it. Will a song be playing? Will family be standing near by or will it just be the two of you?

Photo by Milton Yin
Purvi Tank in a pre-wedding Hindu prayer, or *puja* ceremony.

One Month in Advance
Check and double check…

- By now, your pre-wedding ceremonies may have even started!
- Finalize reception seating charts and print place cards.
- Schedule final meetings at venues and with vendors to confirm arrangements.
- Finalize a program, and have them printed.
- Determine a personal wedding morning schedule (What time will you wake up? When does hair and makeup start? When will you leave the house?).
- Confirm transportation and accommodation arrangements for all out-of-town guests
- Organize all your wedding extras: favors, gifts, garlands, props for each event (i.e *dholkis* for a sangeet, or *dandia sticks* for a *raas-garba*) and make sure everything is accessible for the day they're needed.
- Confirm your honeymoon details and pack your honeymoon luggage.
- Arrange any welcome baskets or goodies for out-of-town guests

One Week in Advance
Let the festivities begin…

- Final fittings for wedding day attire. Have a seamstresses on-hand to make any alterations.
- Start receiving out-of-town guests.
- Enjoy your pre-wedding ceremonies.

Day of Wedding
Breathe in, breathe out…

- Let the arrangements take care of themselves. Enjoy the company of your guests who have made an effort to attend your special weekend. Remind your parents to relax and enjoy the wedding as well.
- Sit back, be beautiful, and don't forget to smile…

Special thanks to Sara Muchnick of Engaging Affairs, in Virginia for her helpful planning tips.

Photo by Milton Yin
Sit back and enjoy your wedding day.

What's Their Story?

Past Lives. Granted, it can be a touchy subject to dig too deep into anyone's past—especially your parents'—but I can't help but be fascinated by the marriage stories of previous generations. And I'm surprised how many people don't know their parents' wedding story. My parents have a somewhat different story than most Indian couples of their age, having met and married in America. In my father's family, most of his siblings had arranged marriages in India and later, one-by-one, made the move to America landing in places as seemingly obscure as West Virginia. They casually recap their histories to me, as if it were nothing to meet, marry, then pack up and move away to another country when they were younger. It seems so long ago, like another lifetime. But I look at them and imagine what they were like when they were my age, when they were unmarried and later as they became young wives and husbands.

I think about a photograph that my best friend kept in her bedroom—a photograph of her mother, young and newly married in Amritsar, India. In the photo, she wears a white, flowing *kurta* and her uncut hair softly unwinds out of a braid. Lounging on a sofa, smiling as if she was holding back her laughter, the moment is romantic and almost dream-like. She is a woman in love. Her face is relaxed and she is untouched by the rocky path she and her husband would lead as they set off to make a life in Manhattan.

Do you know your parent's wedding story? What were they like when they were your age? When they got married? What difficulties did they have in their first weeks of marriage? What about some of your family members, your aunts and uncles? As you approach marriage yourself, there's no better time to find out your parents' wedding story if you don't already know it. Here are some questions to consider as you get your conversation started:

- How did your parents meet?
- How did they decide to get married?
- How long did they know each other before they got married?
- How many years ago did they marry?
- Where was the wedding? Where was the reception?
- Who planned their wedding?
- Which family members played the biggest roles in their wedding?
- How many people attended the wedding?
- What did their wedding outfits look like?
- What did they eat on their wedding day?
- What is their favorite memory from the day?
- How soon after they married did they move to America?
- Did they both want to move to America?
- How is your wedding going to be different from theirs? And how will it be similar?

Words of Wisdom

When I close my eyes and think back to my wedding I think of…

"… all my family and friends running around to complete last minute tasks to make everything perfect and it made me notice how many amazing people I had around me.

–Joti Poonia, May 30, 2009, Silver Spring, MD

"… the greatest time in my life, surrounded by the people I love the most in the world."

–Eena Sidhu, June 27, 2009, Waldorf, MD

"… family and how beautiful and loved I felt. And also the awesome decorations and how beautiful the venue looked.

–Chinar Desai, August 22, 2009, Springfield, PA

"… the smile on my husband's face when I first walked into the ceremony."

–Bincy Puthenmadathi, August 11, 2007, Randolph, NJ

"… a haze of colors, tears, and smiles."

–Jenny Ahuja, Sikh ceremony and reception, November 26, 2006, Baltimore, MD, and Catholic wedding and reception, December 2, 2006, Miami, FL

"… snapshots of memories from my wedding, shopping with my parents in India, and all that they have done to make my wedding what I have always wanted to when I departed my house with a realization that I was officially married."

–Poonam Rakkar, April 11, 2009, Modesto, CA

"… our families getting together, everyone being happy, and the food!"

–Meghana Acharya, June 6, 2009, San Ramon, CA

"I think it was the happiest day of my life, the day I married someone who I'd share priceless life lessons with, grow as an individual with, have children with, and grow old with."

–Simi Grewal-Singh, February 10, 2007, Fremont, CA

"... the first glimpse I took of our ballroom that was so romantic and glamorous. The room had dangling chandeliers, exotic white flowers with gold accents, crystals, and candlelight, which created a dreamy fairy tale setting."

–Nazia Khan, July 18, 2008, Chicago, IL

"... the time I got to share with my family and my new family. It was the first time everyone got to spend time together and enjoy each other's company, while welcoming us to each other's family! Also, the biggest thing is spending each and every moment of the wedding and reception with my husband."

–Kajal Patel, Saturday June 27, 2009, Cherry Hill, NJ

"... my husband/family/friends, all the beautiful and meaningful rituals, and CELEBRATING. *Can't forget the beautiful outfits/jewelry!"*

–Ameeta Singh, June 3, 2006, Fairfax, VA

"... how calm I was considering it was one of the biggest moments of my life to date."

–Navleen Sandhu, October 29, 2005, Gaithersburg, MD

"... how I've never been so nervous for anything in my life, but the moment I finally made it to the stage and my future hubby held my hand, I knew I got my happily ever after!"

–Tanisha Gulhar, May 24, 2008, Reston Town Center, VA

Section II: Make it Yours

Photo by Robert Isacson
Kavi Thakrar, pre-wedding ceremony

Stationary: Brand Your Wedding
It all starts with a date…

Traditionally in India, the parents of the bride and groom would hand-deliver wedding invitations to each family member and to close friends. The invitation would usually be accompanied by a box of fresh *mithai*, sweets. Nothing says, "let's get this party started" better than a personal invitation and some sweet treats. Nowadays, with friends and relatives spread out all over the world, hand delivery is an unrealistic hope for most couples. But that doesn't mean your invitation can't still reflect a personal charm.

Your wedding stationary is an expression of the tone and style of your wedding and presents your first official statement announcing your marriage. Stationary goes beyond just invitations and can include Save the Date cards, programs, table placements, menu cards, and thank you cards, so think ahead and choose a concept early on that can be incorporated across your wedding events. "You're creating a visual language for your wedding. You're branding your wedding with a design or motif that can work as your décor theme," says Saima Khan of Saima Says Designs.

Design: When you create the look and feel of your invitation, find inspiration from your heritage, family traditions, the season, the venue, your outfits, or your theme, says Saima. Will your wedding be indoors or outdoors? Is it a destination wedding? Will your events be traditional or a fusion of cultures? Is there a theme?

"Don't be afraid of color," says Saima, who encourages couples to experiment with different color palettes. "Couples worry that if they stray from the traditional red and gold combination, they'll lose the festive, traditional feel of their events. It's just not the case," she says.

Invitation photographs courtesy Saima Says Designs
Experiment with colors and try to create a visual language for your wedding, says designer Saima Khan.

Play with textures like different papers, fabrics, or even wood and Plexiglas, or consider boxed invitations and invitations written out on a scrolls. Saima used braided bamboo stalk to back an invitation to a beach ceremony, and wood veneer for a rustic fall wedding. Add texture to paper invitations with engraving and letterpress printing for the text. Embellishments like crystals, beads, lace, ribbons, and sashes can add a dramatic dimension to your announcements.

But keep in mind, multiple colors, embellishments, fabrics, and thick card stock, will affect the price point of your invitations, so consider your budget if it's a concern.

Organization: Don't forget that the purpose of an invitation, especially for South Asian weddings that have multiple events, is to lay out and organize your wedding schedule for your guests. Pocket-fold invitations are often the best option when you have multiple events, allowing you to list each event on a separate card. Insert cards give you the flexibility to choose which events each guest will be invited to.

Mailing Labels: You've taken the time to design a beautiful invitation, so don't ruin it by sticking a white address label to the outside of the envelope, says Saima. Addresses can be printed on the envelope, or you can address each invitation by hand to add an extra personal touch.

Wording: Language etiquette varies by family, but the host of each event should be acknowledged on the invitation. Typically, the parents and grandparents are recognized on invitations for ceremonies and receptions, while siblings are named as hosts for pre-wedding events like sangeets.

Made in India: For those who travel abroad for wedding shopping, invitations are usually on the shopping list. Printing prices are much cheaper abroad and you'll have a wide selection to choose from. But, if you order invitations while you're abroad, go prepared. Be ready to give the printer exact details of the wedding (date, time, location, family names) when you're ordering the cards. Coordinate invitation language with your fiancé before you go abroad. Invitations directly from India are also available online.

The Importance of Programs: With explanations of your ceremonies and a schedule of your events, programs capture the essence of a wedding and can be the best souvenir of your day. Booklet or quad-fold style programs can give you enough space to explain the who's who and what's what of the event.

Programs are an invaluable favor to your guests, organizing and making sense of the rituals of your day.

Pre-Wedding Festivities

Indian life is narrated by song. For every milestone in life, folk songs accompany rites of passage. It's no surprise that across the many South Asian cultures, song and dance are performed before, during, and after weddings.

Religious ceremonies usually kick off the series of wedding events. Once initial religious functions are complete and a tone is set for a blessed wedding, musically driven events like dholki nights, sangeets, or garbas lead up to the wedding day depending on culture and family traditions. These musical celebrations are sometimes as elaborate and large scale as the wedding reception itself. But at the heart of these events is a sense of closeness, and the songs shared at these events tell stories of marriage and new relationships. Some songs share advice of how to adjust to married life while others poke fun at the in-laws. These events used to be for women only, but today, though women still tend to lead the singing and dancing, men attend these celebrations, too.

Mehndi ceremonies where henna is applied on the bride and her female friends and relatives is a major pre-wedding ceremony (see page 100 for more about mehndi.)

Photos by Milton Yin
Purvi launches into garba dance, swaying, spinning, and flowing on the eve of her wedding.

Photo by Milton Yin
In an outdoor *garba* in California, guests danced in an open courtyard, whirling around a fountain dotted with candles.

Photo by Paul Barnett
A bride holds a pot lined with lights above her head during *jaago,* a ceremony meant to awaken, or kick off, the wedding celebrations.

Photo by Paul Barnett
An 'aunty' drums a *dholki* at a sangeet party.

Across many South Asian cultures, during beautification ceremonies, which are more intimate events for family and close friends, *haldi,* a yellow tumeric paste, is applied on both the bride and groom in their respective homes. Applying haldi is meant to give skin a radiant glow, and the ceremony is meant to be fun and lighthearted. In some pre-wedding ceremonies, the adorning of the bride begins, like in the Punjabi *choora* custom, when the bride's mother's brothers put traditional choora, red and cream bridal bangles, on the bride.

Photo by CB Art Photography/Chandrakant Patel
Haldi ceremony

Baraat: The Groom's Arrival
Make an Entrance

The baraat procession is the grand entrance a groom and his family make when they arrive to the wedding. In the days of jeweled maharajas long ago, elite grooms in India would journey to the bride's house on elephant, surrounded by a massive entourage of relatives and friends and heralded by drum and brass bands. The procession celebrated the groom's journey to the bride's home where he would marry her and take her back with him. Though that tradition has been slightly pared down in America, the groom's arrival is still a matter of joyful fanfare and is marked with music and dancing, even if it may be in a temple or hotel parking lot. It's common today for a groom to arrive on horseback, and some grooms even on elephant.

Horse and carriage companies across the country have caught on to the tradition and are well booked for Indian weddings. Some even supply decorative garb for the horse, like sequined drapes and beaded headpieces.

"Our horse was double booked," said Puja Pandya of Maryland. Her July 7, 2007, wedding took place at the Baltimore Waterfront Marriot, and luckily her fiancé, Rajiv, had just enough time to arrive on horseback to the waterfront promenade before the tame white horse was taken off to it's next gig.

As the groom's procession heads toward his wedding ceremony, the groom's face is usually hidden with a *sehra*, a decorative headpiece of cascading beads, threads, or flowers. The bride's family awaits the groom's arrival and welcomes his guests with warm greetings. In some traditions, like Gujurati tradition, the mother of the bride playfully pinches the groom's nose as she welcomes him.

Photo by Yogi Patel, Global Photography LA
Anurag arrives on horseback

Photo by Paul Barnett
The groom looks out from under his *sehra*.

Photo by Glenn Barnett
Sisters and female relatives of the groom tie decorations
on the horse before the baraat procession begins.

47

Photo by Paul Barnett

Photo by CB ART PHOTOGRAPHY / Chandrakant Patel
Grooms of Indian royalty arrived at their weddings on elephant.
Though a rare entrance nowadays, the trend is slowly picking up.

48

Photo by CB ART PHOTOGRAPHY / Chandrakant Patel

Photo by Yogi Patel, Global Photography LA
Dhol player at a baraat

49

Photo by Dallan Photography
Omna and Koushik Bhattacharya married on August 30, 2008,
at the Landsdowne Resort in Virginia.

Your Ceremony: Know Your Rites

Please note: The following explanations of religious ceremonies were written based on research and conversations with families who have recently hosted weddings according to their faith. Ceremonies vary by culture, region, and family so please consult with your family and your religious officiate for further explanation and understanding of your religious practices. The following interpretations offer a general framework and should only be used as a first step to further researching your rituals.

Photo by Yogi Patel of Global Photography LA
Seated at the mandap with family beside them, Neha and Anurag follow the instructions given by their pandit.

Hindu Ceremonies

Marriage is considered one of the most important of the *samskara*s, or life-cycles, in the Hindu tradition—it is the joining of two families in a sacred bond. There are many variations of the Hindu wedding ceremony, as it differs by region, caste, and family tradition. The bride and groom should consult with their family and pandit to better understand the significance of the specific practices of their ceremony.

Hindu wedding ceremonies are lead by a pandit who talks the bride, groom, and their families through the various rituals. The ceremony is conducted partly in Sanskrit, the ancient language of the Vedic texts, and partly in the couple's regional Indian language. Some pandits will translate the Sanskrit into English. Ceremonies can last anywhere from one to three, or more, hours.

Below is a look at the core elements of a Hindu ceremony. The names of the practices vary by language and regional dialect, and again, the sequence and significance of each rite varies. These elements are based on traditions from Northern Indian.

Photo by Glenn Barnett
At the center is the pit where the sacred fire will be lit. Around it are fresh fruit, flowers, and leaves, symbols of nourishment and vitality, and *ghee*, or purified butter, which fuels the fire.

Mahurat: Favorable date. Weeks before the wedding, a pandit is consulted to decide an auspicious or favorable wedding date. Based on Vedic astrology, which factors in the positions of the stars and planets during a person's birth, a wedding date and time that matches both the bride and groom's astrological chart is selected.

Swaagatam: Welcoming of the groom. The bride's family and friends welcome the baraat (the groom's party). The bride's mother may perform *aarti*, a Hindu ritual of blessing, in this case blessing the groom. The father of the bride may apply a *tilak* (red dot) on his forehead, as a gesture of blessing. The bride's father may offer sweet honey and yogurt to the groom as an expression of welcome. The groom is led to the mandap, the pavilion where the ceremony will take place, and he will await the bride.

Ganesh Pooja: Prayer. In this invocation of Lord Ganesh, God of favorable beginnings and remover of obstacles, the deity's blessings are sought for success, peace, and happiness, and to ensure that the ceremony takes place without impediments.

Photo by Robert Isacson
Lord Ganesh

Photo by Dallan Photography
A red *tilak* is applied to the groom as a blessing.

Mangalaashtak: Arrival of the bride. The bride is led to the mandap. Who escorts her varies by tradition—sometimes the bride's maternal uncle will bring her; sometimes its her brothers or female relatives and friends. In some traditions, a white cloth is held in front of the groom so the couple cannot see each other until she arrives to the mandap.

Photo by Milton Yin
Some brides are carried out to the mandap on a platform, or *palanquin*, by their brothers and male relatives.

Photo by Robert Isacson
Before the ceremony begins, at the mandap a white cloth separates Kavi and Maria like a curtain until the pandit completes a mantra.

Jaimaala: Exchanging of garlands. Facing each other, the bride and groom exchange flower garlands, indicating they accept each other for marriage. Sometimes, in a playful show, the bride and groom compete to see who can put the garland on the other first. Male relatives of both the bride and groom will lift them up; whoever is lifted higher usually has the advantage to swap garlands first.

Punyah Wachan: Guests' blessings. Guests are asked to bless the couple as the pandit recites a mantra.

Kanyadan: Giving away the bride. The bride's father gives her hand to the groom as an expression of entrusting his daughter to the groom, and consenting their union.

Havan: Lighting the Holy Fire. The pandit lights the sacred fire, which is meant to invoke *Agni,* the God of fire, who will bear witness to the union. Agni, the great protector against evil, is also a symbol of purity and sacrifice.

Rajaham: Sacrifice to the Fire. The bride and groom offer ghee, puffed rice, and sandalwood to the fire, in a gesture of sacrifice and partnership. Prayers are offered for a long life, strong health, and prosperity.

Gath Bandhan: Tying of the Knot. Depending on tradition, a family member ties a knot using the bride and groom's garments, symbolizing their union.

Mangal phere: Circle the Holy Fire. The climax of the Hindu wedding ceremony, the couple walks in a clockwise direction around the sacred fire. In some traditions, the couple circles the fire four times, whereas in other cultures they circle the fire seven times. A very general interpretation of the revolutions is that they represent four spiritual goals of life:

Dharma: righteousness
Artha: wealth and prosperity
Kamma: desire, energy, and passion for life
Moksha: detachment from worldly things

Photo by Robert Isacson
The pandit adds *ghee* (purified butter) to fuel the sacred fire.

Photo by Robert Isacson
Kavi and Maria take turns adding puffed rice and sandalwood to the fire, signifying a shared sacrifice to the holy fire.

Photo by CB ART PHOTOGRAPHY / Chandrakant Patel
Neil and Shilpi performing Rajaham, sacrifice to the Fire.

Photo by Robert Isacson
Maria leads Kavi in the last of four revolutions around the sacred fire. This couple chose a contemporary mandap design, using birchwood and fresh flowers to create a light and airy pavilion. The mandap was designed by Elegant Affairs.

57

Satapadi: The First Seven Steps. The couple walks seven steps together, their first steps as a married unit. Seven bunches of rice are placed in a row on the ground with a coin on top of each. The bride places her right toe on each heap of rice, each step representing another vow. There are many interpretations of what each step represents, one example:

Step 1: Share in the responsibility of the home
Step 2: Fill our hearts with strength and courage
Step 3: Prosper and share our worldly goods
Step 4: Fill our hearts with love, peace, happiness, and spiritual values
Step 5: Be blessed with loving children
Step 6: Attain self-restraint and longevity
Step 7: Be best friends and eternal partners

Jalastnchana: Blessing. The parents of both the bride and groom bless the couple by dipping a rose in water and sprinkling it over the couple.

Sindhoor: The groom dots *sindhoor*, a red powder, on the bride's forehead or in the parting of her hair, to signify her newly married status. Sindhoor is only worn by married women, and is first worn when the groom applies it to the bride. The groom then ties a *shankha*, a sacred bracelet, on the bride's wrist that also signifies she is married.

Mangal sutra: The groom puts this sacred, black beaded necklace around the bride, a symbol of their union and a tradition similar to putting on a wedding ring.

Photo by Milton Yin
In the *Saptapadi* ceremony, the bride will touch seven mounds of rice that are lined on the ground.

Ashirvad: Congratulations and blessing. The newlyweds touch the feet of both sets of parents, asking for their blessing and also showing their respect for their elders. After the parents give their blessings, guests approach the couple, sometimes showering them with flowers, and offer their congratulations and blessings.

Photo by Robert Isacson
Maria's male relatives playfully twist Kavi's ears, as a reminder to him to care for his new wife. In some languages this is called, *kaan pileei*.

Photo by AISM Photography
In some traditions, the brother of the bride twists the groom's toe as he walks around the fire, until the groom pays up to complete the ceremony.

Sikh Weddings

*"They are not said to be husband and wife, who merely sit together.
Rather they alone are called husband and wife, who have one soul in two bodies."*

–Guru Amar Das, Pauri, pg. 788

Photo by Paul Barnett
Seated on the ground, the bride and groom face the Guru Granth Sahib, the Sikh holy text.

The marriage ceremony of the Sikh faith is called *Anand Karaj,* which translates to "blissful union" or "blissful ceremony." Marriage in the Sikh faith is considered a pairing of two equals, and a spiritual union of two souls. Caste, social status, and astrology hold no significance in Sikh marriages. The Anand Karaj ceremony takes place at the *Gurdwara,* the Sikh temple, and is usually officiated by the *granthi,* the gurdwara's caretaker of the Sikh holy text, the *Sri Guru Granth Sahib.* Sikh ceremonies typically take place in the morning and last a few hours from the arrival of the baraat until the serving of *langar,* a meal after the service. One example of a Sikh wedding is as follows:

Arrival of the Baraat: The bride's family and guests wait outside the gurdwara to welcome the groom and his family. A short *ardaas* prayer is followed by a *milni* ceremony, a warm and official introduction of the two families. Before proceeding into the gurdwara, the bride's family and friends, usually led by her sister, will play a cheeky game at the door and forbid the groom from entering unless he pays up. Breakfast, snacks, and tea are offered before the ceremony begins.

Photo by Paul Barnett
After playful negotiations, the bride's sister hands the groom wobbly scissors to cut through and enter into the gurdwara.

Photo by Glenn Barnett
Kabir Kamboh arrives to the gurdwara on horseback, peaking his face through the *sehra.*

Photo by Paul Barnett
The father of the bride hands his daughter the *palla*. The couple will hold onto the scarf as they walk around the Guru Granth Sahib.

Anand Karaj: Guests fill up the *diwan* hall where the ceremony will take place as *kirtan*, religious hymns, are sung by *raagis*. The groom sits at the front and awaits the bride to enter. His *sehra*, the decorated headpiece he wears during the baraat, should be removed as soon as he arrives in the diwan hall. The bride is later walked in by her family, usually her close female relatives and friends. The bride will sit beside the groom and the ceremony begins when only the bride, groom, and their parents stand up for an ardaas prayer, indicating that both families agree to the marriage.

After ardaas, the bride's father hands one end of the *palla,* a scarf worn by the groom, to the bride, as a symbolic gesture of joining the couple, and giving away the bride to the groom. Then, the granthi will read aloud the first stanza of the *laavan*, the Sikh wedding hymns. After the stanza is completed, the couple will bow down in front of the Guru Granth Sahib, stand up, and walk clockwise around the Guru Granth Sahib as raagis sing out the stanza. The rotation is called a *phera*. The bride follows the groom, and both hold onto the palla. The couple will bow down in front of the Guru Granth Sahib after the rotation. This process is repeated for all four stanzas.

Photo by Paul Barnett
The holy text of the Sikh religion

Photo by Paul Barnett

Photo by Paul Barnett
Palla in hand, the couple circles the Guru Granth Sahib as *raagis* sing a stanza of a *laav* hymn.

The four stanzas of the *laavan* outline a spiritual progression that begins by embracing the Guru's guidance, meditating the Divine name, and ultimately attaining a true and blissful union with God. The symbolic blending of two souls in this ceremony represents a greater spiritual path, a longing to become one with God.

Below are translations of *only the first line* of each stanza.

The First Laav Hymn[1]:

Har peh-larr-ee laav par-vir-tee karam drirr-aa-i-aa bal raam jeeo

In the first round of the marriage ceremony, the Lord sets out His Instructions for performing the daily duties of married life.

The Second Laav Hymn:

Har dooj-rree laav satigur purakh milaa-i-aa bal raam jeeo

In the second round of the marriage ceremony, the Lord leads one to meet the True Guru, the Primal Being.

The Third Laav Hymn:

Har tee-jarr-ee laav man chaao bha-i-aa bai-raag-ee-aa bal raam jeeo

In the third round of the marriage ceremony, the mind is filled with divine love.

The Fourth Laav Hymn:

Har chou-tha-rree laav man sehaj bha-i-aa har paa-i-aa bal raam jeeo

In the fourth round of the marriage ceremony, the mind becomes peaceful having found the Lord.

Etiquette when attending a ceremony at the gurdwara:

As you enter the gurdwara you'll be asked to remove your shoes, a sign of respect. There will be a designated area for you to leave your shoes while you're in the gurdwara.

When you enter the diwan hall, the room where the holy book rests, both males and females are expected to cover their head, so be sure to bring a scarf. Covering your head is a sign of respect when you're in the presence of the holy book. Extra scarves are usually available at gurdwaras in case you forget. Depending on the fabric of the scarf, they can slip off your head, so try to be aware and make sure your head is always covered.

When you enter the diwan hall, you'll walk to the front of the room where the Shri Guru Granth Sahib rests, and you'll bow down, touching your forehead to the ground, as a sign of respect for the holy text. It's customary to make a small offering, but not mandatory.

In the diwan hall, you'll see that males and females sit apart, and on the floor, on opposite sides of the room.

[1] Khalsa, Sukhmandir. *Lavan, the Sikh Wedding Rounds.* (http://sikhism.about.com)

Christian Wedding
According to the Malankara Orthodox Syrian Church

In a beautiful mix of culture and faith, the sacred rite of Holy Matrimony according to the Christian faith blends regional practices with holy doctrine. As with other religious services, there are variations in rituals between different denominations.

In the Malankara Orthodox Syrian Church, weddings blend South Indian customs with Biblical traditions from the Old Testament and teachings from the New Testament. Wedding ceremonies take place in a church and are officiated by a priest, though a deacon may also preside. Ceremonies are straightforward in ritual, and usually last no more than an hour or two. Within the Mar Thoma denomination, similar to the Orthodox faith, the priest includes chants in the Malayalee language and lively choirs sing during the ceremony.

Photo courtesy Bincy Jacob Puthenmadathil
Bincy and Binoy Puthenmadathil

Photo by Paul Barnett
The groom, Mat Alexander, a deacon in the Malankara Syrian Orthodox Church, stands at the altar before his wedding ceremony begins.

Photo by Paul Barnett
Manju joins her fiancé at the altar

Following the processional of the wedding party and the seating of the parents, the father of the bride walks her down the aisle where the groom awaits her at the altar. Some brides choose to wear white wedding gowns, and others a white silk sari embroidered with gold plated threads. If she wears a sari, she may cover her head as a sign of modesty.

The defining services of the ceremony are as follows:

The Blessing of the Rings: In this first service, the Lord is asked to bless the rings and bind the two into one. The couple exchanges vows and rings.

The Blessing of the Crown: In this second service, the couple is crowned as the righteous man and wife of a new Christian home. Gold necklaces with a cross pendant are first blessed by the priest and then used to symbolically crown the couple.

The Blessing of the Crown is followed by the tying of the *minnu*, a necklace with a small gold pendant that hangs on a cord made of seven threads. The threads are pulled from a wedding sari that will be given to the bride called a

manthrakodi. In South Indian Hindu traditions, the minnu is called a *taali* and is tied as a *mangal sutra*. The groom ties the minnu around the neck of the bride as a vow of eternal commitment to the bride. After he ties the necklace, the manthrakodi, or wedding sari from the groom to the bride, is placed on the bride's head. The priest blesses the couple.

Photo by Paul Barnett
The bride is given a wedding sari from the groom's family called the manthrakodi. The sari is placed over her head during the ceremony.

Photo by Paul Barnett
In the Crowning ceremony, the priest blesses the bride and groom and symbolically crowns them by touching a gold necklace to their head.

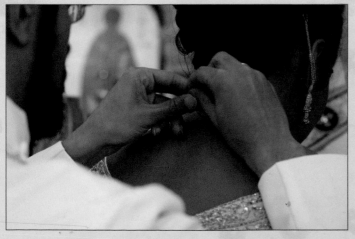

Photo by Paul Barnett
Mat ties the *minnu* around Manju. The minnu necklace is made from seven threads from a wedding sari that the groom gives the bride.

Photo by Paul Barnett
The bride and groom sign an official register in front of the congregation, signifying their mutual consent to the marriage.

69

The sister of the groom now takes the place of the maid of honor who had been standing beside the bride, signifying that she will now care for the bride as the newest member of the family. The couple signs the register in front of the congregation, publicly indicating that both bride and groom accept this union.

The couple is announced as husband and wife after the priest gives a sermon about the responsibilities of marriage.

The ceremony is followed by a meal and later by a reception.

Photo by Paul Barnett
Officially married…

Photo by Paul Barnett
Manju and Mat leave church hand-in-hand as newlyweds.

70

Photo by Paul Barnett

Photos courtesy Omar Uddin
Hina and Omar married in December 2006

Muslim Traditions

Muslim weddings are both private and grand affairs. They are weighted with the solemn promise of a marriage contract but stylishly festive. *Dholki* and mehndi nights booming with lighthearted music lead up to the wedding and reception. Like with other South Asian traditions, there are variations of practices and of religious interpretations, but some of the core elements of a South Asian Muslim wedding are as follows:

Mangni: The groom's side officially asks for the bride's hand in marriage at the bride's house. Rings are sometimes exchanged during this engagement ceremony or sometimes exchanged after the *nikaah*.

Mayoon Haldi: A yellow turmeric paste. Applied on the bride and groom in their respective homes. Haldi is considered a skin beautifier, as it is meant to make the skin glow. During the mayoon, the bride typically wears a *peela jorda*, or a yellow outfit, that is given to her by the groom's family. After friends and relatives take turns applying *haldi* to the bride's skin, she bathes it off.

Mehndi: The groom's family brings decorated trays of mehndi to the bride's event. In some traditions, the bride holds a leaf in her hand and married women take turns adding a dot of mehndi to the leaf (so the henna doesn't stain her hand) in a gesture of blessing her. Henna designs are applied to the bride's hands and feet, as well as on the hands of her female family and friends. The mehndi takes place a day or two before the wedding and is an integral and very festive pre-wedding event with lively music and dance. (Read more about mehndi on page 40.)

Baraat: Sometimes before the *nikaah*, and sometimes before the *rukshat*, the groom and his guests arrive in a lively *baraat* procession. The groom wears a *sehra* headpiece made of flowers. They are welcomed by the bride's family and sometimes offered sweet *sharbaat*. (Read more about the *baraat* on page 44.)

Nikaah: The defining marriage ceremony in the Muslim tradition is called the nikaah in the Urdu language. The nikaah is an intimate ceremony and can sometimes even take place during the mehndi or mayoon. The ceremony is officiated by a *maulvi*, a priest, and close family members, especially the *walis*, or fathers of the bride and groom, witness the ceremony. The bride and groom sit in separate rooms or are divided by a *pardah*, a curtain-like cloth, during the ceremony. Verses from the Quran are read aloud by the maulvi, and he then asks both the bride and groom if they consent to the marriage in a tradition called the *Ijab-e-Qubul*. To accept, the bride and groom will each say, "*qubul*" three times after he asks for their acceptance. The maulvi also asks the bride if she accepts the *mehr* or the wedding gift that is given to the bride's family from the groom's parents.

Upon the couple's acceptance of the marriage, the bride and groom sign the *nikaah-naama*, an official contract of marriage. The *walis* and *maulvi* also sign this document.

Rukshat: The bride officially leaves her parents' house with the groom. In some traditions, the bride is meant to visit her parents home again after four days.

Dressed in a *peela jorda*, a yellow outfit, Hina arrives to her *mayou* or *mayoon* ceremony where friends and family will dot *haldi*, a yellow tumeric paste, on her face.

Face covered in *haldi*, Hina smiles with her fiancé Omar two nights before their wedding.

During the *nikaah*, an imam asks the bride, Hina, if she accepts the marriage proposal.

Both bride and groom must sign the *nikaah-naama*, an official marriage contract.

Surrounded by family and friends, the couple exchanges rings.

Valima: The groom's family throws a reception party to celebrate the newlyweds. This is usually a major event, and unlike the *nikaah,* which is more private and intimate in nature for just the family, the valima is a public party. As with other receptions, the valima isn't complete without a grand meal.

Doli or Bidai

Doli or *bidai is the* bride's departure. This is one of the most emotional aspects of the wedding ceremony. Here, the bride, now married, officially leaves her parents' house and goes with her husband to her new family. In some traditions, as the bride leaves the house she throws handfuls of rice behind her, as a gesture to symbolize that she hopes her parents' house is always full with nourishment and prosperity. As the bride leaves to go with her husband, she is sometimes carried away in a doli, a carriage platform held up by her brothers. Once she sits in the car with her husband, often her brothers will push the car as it sets off, in their last act of giving her away. While the ceremony is emotional in its meaning, often in Indian American weddings, the bride doesn't go to her husband's families house immediately after the wedding, and instead sees all her guests a few hours later at the reception.

Photo by Yogi Patel, Global Photography LA
Officially married, Anurag and Neha leave together as husband and wife.

Words of Wisdom

My wedding planning advice to a bride or couple would be…

"Make compromises, be organized, and try to enjoy the process, because all of the hard work culminates to one day that you want to remember forever."

–Omna Kohli, August 30, 2008, Lansdowne, VA

"Don't take things too seriously. Remember to have fun in the midst of all the planning."

–Eena Sidhu, June 27, 2009, Waldorf, MD

"Don't be stressed on the day of the wedding. Let others take care of the details. You have done all you can up to this point and now it's your day to enjoy the hard work of all the planning and thought you put into your wedding. One word—delegate! Let others help you and trust that they will do a good job. Coming from a complete, anal bridezilla …this is easier said than done.

–Chinar Desai, August 22, 2009, Springfield, PA

"Know what you want as a couple because you will get opinions and advice from everyone, so its important to know what you as a couple want so that your wedding is everything that you both are hoping for. Also, its important to realize that no matter how much time, energy, and meticulous planning you put into your wedding, sometimes things might not work out the way you hoped/planned, so its important to have an open mind and not sweat the details, otherwise you will miss out on enjoying that moment which you can never get back."

–Bincy Puthenmadathi, August 11, 2007, Randolph, NJ

"Think of the honeymoon as the vacation from being full time party planners."

–Jenny Ahuja, Sikh ceremony and reception, November 26, 2006, Baltimore, MD, and Catholic wedding and reception, December 2, 2006, Miami, FL

"…for the couple to enjoy themselves since weddings are very intense and stressful. Its a huge step in anyone's life and should be shared together every step of the way. I was grateful enough to have my husband alongside me planning and enjoying everything with me."

–Poonam Rakkar, April 11, 2009, Modesto, CA

"Start early and start now."

–Meghana Acharya, June 6, 2009, San Ramon, CA

"Don't solicit too much advice. It's your wedding, your day! Do what your heart desires to make it the most memorable event of your life!"

–Rupa Gill, May 16, 2004, Charleston, WV

"... not to sweat the small stuff: let your families and friends enjoy some of the planning, and don't fight about minuscule details that won't matter one year from the wedding date."

–Simi Grewal-Singh, February 10, 2007, Fremont, CA

"Even if you are a 'Do it Yourself' person, you must delegate, or else the planning process will turn into your worst nightmare. Create a circle of close friends, family, professionals, that you trust and can lean on, and let them help with all the time consuming details so you can sit back, relax, and enjoy.

–Nazia Khan, July 18, 2008, Chicago, IL

"Don't sweat the small stuff. Planning an Indian wedding specifically is full of thousands of details and there are bound to be a few snafus along the way. Keep in mind the reason you are doing all of this—it's to celebrate your love together!"

Kajal Patel, June 27, 2009, Cherry Hill, NJ

"Enjoy every moment, don't sweat the small stuff. Take as much help from family and friends as you can, don't take on too much on your own."

–Ameeta Singh, June 3, 2006, Fairfax, VA

"Have fun with it. Otherwise it will seem like an overwhelming and daunting task."

–Navleen Sandhu, October 29, 2005, Gaithersburg, MD.

"If you can make it through this process you can make it through anything! Enjoy every second of it—you never get it back!"

–Tanisha Gulhar, May 24, 2008, Reston Town Center, VA

Section III: All That Glitters

Photo Courtesy Ziba Beauty Salons

On Beauty

Whether your bridal vibe is Bollywood glamour or California cool, your makeup is a defining element of your wedding day style. A good makeup job will enhance your best features to achieve a dramatic, once-in-a-lifetime look.

Finding your makeup artist can be as easy as asking a few of your favorite brides for recommendations. If you liked their look, give their makeup artist a call. Ask to see the artist's portfolio and maybe get in touch with a few of their previous clients. You want someone as reliable and pleasant as they are talented. Always ask for a trial consultation. Build a relationship with your stylist so you feel at ease trusting them on your special day.

A good makeup job will enhance your best features to achieve a dramatic, once-in-a-lifetime look.

Photo by AISM Photography
Mishty Kapoor. Makeup and styling by
Suman Khosla, Virginia

Fresh Faced: "But I want to look natural." Sure, you want to be able to recognize yourself in the mirror on your wedding day, but don't shy away from wearing more makeup than you typically do. As the bride, you should look outstanding, and it takes careful planning and application of makeup to give the face a fresh, natural glow that doesn't appear washed out on camera.

Skin Care: Do your part and invest time into beauty preparations well in advance. If you want skin that glows on your big day, you'll need to start early. Hydrate your skin with daily water intake and cleanse and pamper your skin with facials or gently exfoliate it weekly at home with Epsom salt and rose water.

For those dark circles around the eyes that plague so many of us, don't look for quick fixes, says Sumita Batra of Ziba Beauty. "You can't buy a miracle in a bottle, so don't fall for any gimmicks," she says. To remedy the purple, blue, and black hues that might ring around your eyes, drink plenty of water for at least two months leading up to your wedding, and get as much sleep as you can. Chilled cucumbers on the eyes can help reduce puffiness.

Take the time to test and find the right skin care line that works for you. "I don't recommend mixing and matching brands. Be consistent with one skin care regimen because products in a line are formulated to work with each other," says Batra.

You are what you eat, so lay off the samosas and fried foods to minimize oily skin. Pack your diet with fresh fruits and vegetables, especially the days just before your wedding.

Color Palette: "Love your complexion," says Suman Patel of Ziba Beauty. Use foundations and concealers that complement the natural color of your skin. A foundation that is too light won't make you look fair, she says. Rather, it's a sure bet that you'll get a "caked-on effect." She says, "Your face will look fake and unnatural."

Don't feel you have to match your make up to your outfit. Instead, look for contrasting colors that complement your skin and pull out hints of your outfit. Darker lipsticks may age you in photos, so try on shaded glosses instead of deep maroons and burgundies that might match your outfits.

Be mindful of the lighting at your events. Adjust your makeup to work in the daylight or under different tints at your evening events. Work with your photographer and makeup artist to understand what lighting best defines and contours your features for your portrait shots.

Photo by Paul Barnett

Photo by Dallan Photography
Omna Bhattacharya. Make-up and styling
by Suman Khosla, Virginia

Photo by Dallan Photography
Omna Bhattacharya. Make-up and styling by Suman Khosla, Virginia

Dramatize: False eyelashes are a must to accentuate your eyes, says Patel. But one size doesn't fit all, so test them out first. If your eyes are already large, you may only need the lashes at the corners and tips of your lids. Use eyelash glue to fix them on, and carry a tube of glue with you in case of a lash emergency.

Bridal bindis dotted above your eyebrows will also add a dramatic and traditional touch to your face.

Don't Leave Home Without It: Assign a bridesmaid, or someone close to you, to carry a goody bag of beauty products that you'll likely need throughout the events to keep your look fresh. Make sure to have at least these items on hand and think about what else you might need have handy:

Safety pins
Eyelash glue (if you're fluttering false lashes)
Blotting paper, because you will get oily
Breath mints are a must
Lip gloss

Photo by AISM Photography
Bridal *bindis* and a *tikka*
hairpiece create a traditional,
glamorous look,

*All the elements of your bridal
look should flow together, says
Patel.*

Make sure to break your shoes in before
your wedding day. The last thing you
need are a few blisters.

The Importance of a Trial: The last thing you want on your wedding day is a beauty malfunction. Once you've decided on a stylist, schedule a long block of time with them to create your full wedding day look. Be prepared to pay for this trial, as a thorough trial can take longer than getting ready on your wedding day.

Try every piece of the wardrobe you plan to wear that day, including your outfit, bra, shoes, and jewelry—especially earrings, which tend to be painfully heavy and uncomfortable. Once your hair is set, walk around. How does your hair feel? Too loose? Too many pins?

Cover your head if you plan to on your wedding day, and walk around. Adjust the draping and pinning as needed. All the elements of your bridal look should flow together, says Patel. Don't forget to take a digital camera with you.

Bridal Party: Don't forget the top name in your bridal party list when you book your hair and makeup—your mother, says bridal stylist Suman Khosla of Virginia. Schedule her hair and makeup earlier than your styling begins, so she'll be free to meet and mingle with guests as you get ready.

Photo by AISM Photography
Daughter and mother-in-law both styled by
Suman Khosla, Virginia

Photo by AISM Photography
Hair, make-up, jewelry… all the elements
should flow together.

Your Wedding Dress and Jewelry

*"By adorning the visible, material body, they also seek to satisfy a universal longing
for the embellishment of its intangible counterpart: the human spirit."*

–Oppi Untract, from *Mehndi: The Timeless Art of Henna Painting*

Beyond aesthetic beauty, the bridal wear of Indian weddings are exquisite expressions of vitality. Rich brocades and heavy silks are embellished with hand-placed crystals and *kundan* and fastened with gold plated threads. Traditionally, bridal wear was left to the bride's parents' discretion, and from head to toe she wore a display of the abundance and tradition of her family. But today, Indian American brides are less restricted, and literally have a world of bridal wear options to choose from. And while the traditional bridal hues of red and gold have been sidelined for trendy turquoises and pinks, the striking colors and styles of traditional Indian bridal attire remain a timeless expression of emotion, fertility, and femininity.

Photo by Glenn Barnett
Crowded dressings rooms are common…

"I grew up surrounded by textiles," says Priti Malhotra. A super-mom and business-woman by day, Priti packs her high-energy spirit and creative talents into designing bridal and formal wear for her company, Illusions Designs.

As a young girl, Priti spent her summer vacations with relatives in India and Dubai while her parents continued to work in the States. Reluctant and bored away from home, Priti would find refuge in the fabrics and designs that filled her summer home. "I'd lose myself in my *nani's* (maternal grandmother's) closet. Everyday I'd play with her clothes and try on all her jewelry." To keep her busy, her grandparents enrolled Priti in local sewing classes to pass the summer days. Soon enough, Priti developed the skills that she'd later use to jump-start her career in designing and styling and then to start her own line, Illusions Designs.

Illusions Designs and other Indian American lines like Gurdiya Couture in New York and Shelley Chhabra of Boston offer homegrown designs for Indian bridal attire. These designers provide brides the choice of custom Indian wear without the shopping trip to India.

When designing your outfit, think about the fabrics, embellishments and cut of your outfit. If you know what jewelry you plan to wear, tell your designer so its look and feel can be incorporated into the neckline and overall appearance of the outfit. Think about how you'll need to wear your outfit… will your head be covered for the entire duration of the event? Discuss your ideas with your family… what might seem appropriate and trendy to you might seem disrespectful to your family. Want a backless blouse? You might want to run that by your family. Want to wear a white outfit? Again, you might want to run that by your family. You don't want any surprise reactions.

Photo by Paul Barnett
Both outfits designed by Priti Malhotra

Photo by Yogi Patel, Global Photography LA

Photo by BnB Photography
Designer Prabhleen Bindra, Gurdiya Couture

Brocade silk maroon sherwani self embroidered fabric with
traditional Indian paisleys in swarovski crystal pattern

Photo by BnB Photography
Designer Prabhleen Bindra, Gurdiya Couture

Photo by Milton Yin

Glass bangles, crystal bindis, gold necklaces,
silver anklets, mirrored boxes, pashmeena shawls....
these are a few of my favorite things...

Shopping Abroad

Many Indian American brides take a two-week whirlwind trip to India to shop for their wedding trousseau, but as more Indian boutiques pop up across big cities, brides have the option to custom design their outfits right here in the States. The experience of shopping in India though is one that most brides wouldn't give up, and for good reason. The quality, variety, style, and personal attention you'll receive while shopping for your most memorable outfit is limitless and unparalleled in the subcontinent. Prices are usually cheaper too. With grand bazaars and crowded street stalls at every corner, embroidery, embellishments, and fabrics of every color can be handcrafted into a one-of-a-kind piece just for you.

But—reality check—while I'd like to frame the experience as an enlightening, soul-satisfying vacation back to your ancestral roots, packed with mother-daughter bonding, that wouldn't be the whole truth. Wedding shopping abroad can be overwhelming and not always a retail tourism getaway.

The key to a successful shopping visit is pre-trip bridal research. Likely, when you're in India, you'll be with your mom… and about two-dozen cousins, aunties, friends, and neighbors who want to share your every move while you shop. They probably won't be shy about giving their opinion when they think you look fat, ugly, plain, or gaudy, and aggressive shopkeepers will run circles around you with fabrics of every color and texture. To avoid a bridal meltdown of Indian proportions, it's important to have some idea of what you want. Even if you haven't a clue of what color or style of outfit you want, try to make some preliminary decisions before heading to the stores.

Under the pressure of demanding work schedules, brides can usually only afford a week's worth of vacation days from the office to travel abroad, so set yourself a shopping plan of action. Here are some tips to help you shop with ease, and here's hoping you get to sit back and sip on a "cold drink" while storeowners show you their finest goods.

Know what You Want: Or at least, *have an idea of what you like and don't like*. Be prepared that everyone from the shopkeeper to customers to your shopping entourage will be dishing out their opinions about what you should do. Keep magazine clippings or photos of what you want on hand to show tailors—they can easily reproduce designs.

Photo by Glenn Barnett

97

Know Your Budget: If you're not familiar with shopping in India, shop with a local who can help you negotiate prices and spot a deal (or a scam). Some smaller stores don't offer receipts, and casual purchases on the street add up, so keep a notebook on hand to track how much you spend.

Map it Out: Unless you have the luxury of ample time, don't hop around to too many cities. You don't want to waste time in traffic and travel delays. Your tailor will need time to design and produce your outfits, so plan to shop for your wedding clothes early in the trip. Try on your outfits at least a few days before you have to head back home—the tailor will need time to make final adjustments to your outfit.

Organize Your Wish List: Don't leave home without a shopping list. You're not traveling thousands of

Photo by Glenn Barnett

miles just to buy one outfit. What outfits do you need for other functions? Need outfits for other friends, family, or bridesmaids? Do you have measurements for all the outfits you need? What about accessories? Gifts? Favors? Decorations? Centerpieces? Invitations? See what I mean... travel with a list.

Invitations: If you're planning to order invitations abroad, confirm the details about each event (time, date, location, names) before you meet the printer. Who is hosting each event? How should the invitation be worded? What's the address for each event location? What's your wedding website address?

An Obvious Icebreaker: Maybe this is your first trip to India, or maybe it's your first time back since you were a child. It can be overwhelming to suddenly meet family for the first time or after years of distance. The obvious icebreaker is to talk about weddings—yours of course, but also ask about recent weddings in the family over there. Find out more about your own parents' and grandparents' weddings. Ask for marriage advice... you might be surprised what you learn.

Photo by Glenn Barnett

Photo by Paul Barnett

Mehndi

"From the deserts of North Africa to the villages of northern India, magnificent designs blossom and vanish upon the hands and feet of women as they have for thousands of years."

–Loretta Roome, from *Mehndi: The Timeless Art of Henna Painting*

Photo by CB ART PHOTOGRAPHY / Chandrakant Patel

The darker the mehndi appears on your skin, the more your husband will love you. So they say. I've also heard, the darker the mehndi appears on your skin, the nicer your mother-in-law will treat you.

Well, actually, a number of factors affect the color that mehndi, the Hindi word for henna, will leave on your hands. Take the quality of the henna for example, as well as the application and removal of the henna. But I always hear those predictions at mehndi ceremonies when aunties grip a henna-stained hand as if they are palm readers deciphering the language of color instead of lines.

Ask your family: What does the darkness of the color indicate to them? While you're at it, I've also heard that newly married women aren't supposed to do any work—domestic and otherwise—until all the mehndi fades from their skin. I wonder if your fiancé has anything to say about that?

Photo by Milton Yin

Photo by Milton Yin

Photo by Milton Yin

Photo by Paul Barnett

Photos by Milton Yin

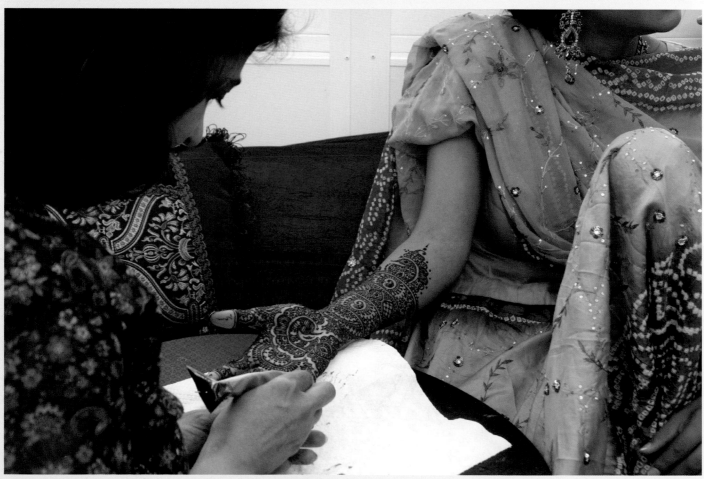

Photo by Paul Barnett
With her mehndi drying, Aman claps along during her sangeet.

Growing up I was that little girl who was first in line to stick my hands out at mehndi ceremonies, eager for peacocks and paisleys to fill my palms. Back then, mehndi ceremonies in my family were small, intimate and in someone's basement. We'd sit on old bed sheets and my aunties would mix together henna paste in plastic bowls and use toothpicks and popsicle sticks to shape designs on our hands. I'd usually be disappointed when an aunty would slop on a maze of thick lines and polka dots across my hands. Did she really just put a smiley face in the center of my palm? More disappointing than the design was the color it'd leave on my skin. I'd do my best to leave the mehndi on for several hours, sometimes tying plastic bags around my hands so I could sleep with it on. But the color it'd leave on my skin was more orange highlighter than dark henna. (Please let my husband love me more than that!) But, despite my many mehndi malfunctions, it has remained my favorite part of weddings. To me, mehndi is deeply feminine and romantic, a silent announcement of celebration. With a long history that dates back to an ancient era of Egyptian pharaohs, I find the ritual of decorating a woman's body with henna beautifully artful.

Mehndi ceremonies in America have come a long way since when I was a little girl. They are typically a core bridal wedding event across the South Asian religious and cultural landscape. Stemming from the Sanskrit word *mendika*, you may have also heard it called *menhadi, mehendi, mehedi*, or *mendi* depending on the language you speak. Mehndi ceremonies are usually a day or two before the wedding, and can be as lavish as a reception, or as intimate as a bridal shower. Hiring a talented bridal mehndi artist in your area is just a Google search away, and quality henna cones are available online or at specialty South Asian stores if you're up for a little DIY.

What is Mehndi?: Mehndi is made from the dried leaves of the henna plant, a Mediterranean shrub. Crushed into powder and then turned into paste, applying mehndi to the body is an ancient practice that has aesthetic appeal, as well as healing and cooling benefits for the skin.

The Henna: Using quality henna is the best way to assure a deep stain on your skin. Find out from your mehndi artist what kind of henna will be used. Do not use black henna, as it will likely burn your skin. You can do a trial on a small section of your hands and feet where you plan to apply the mehndi months before your wedding to test your skin's reaction to the henna and to gauge how long the color will linger on your skin (usually about two weeks.)

The Design: Most mehndi artists have design books and can recommend different patterns and styles for your hands and feet. Designs range from traditional art with peacocks, flowers, elephants, and Raja-Rani scenes to contemporary designs that have a more Arabic influence. Don't forget to incorporate the groom's name into the design you choose so he'll have to search your skin to find his name, *wink wink.*

The Application: Depending on how intricate of a design you want, applying mehndi to your hands, wrists, and up to your elbows can take a few hours, and similarly for your feet and ankles. Once the mehndi has been applied, it should be maintained. As the paste begins to dry on your skin, a simple mixture of lemon juice and sugar should be dabbed onto the mehndi with a cotton ball. The longer you leave the mehndi on your skin, the darker it will stain, so plan to leave it on for at least four hours, and constantly moisten it with the lemon sugar mix.

Photo by Milton Yin

Photo by Milton Yin
As tedious as it can be, it's important to leave the mehndi on for at least four to six hours to get a deep henna stain.

Photo by Milton Yin
Colored glitter, crystals, and other accessories can glam up your henna designs.

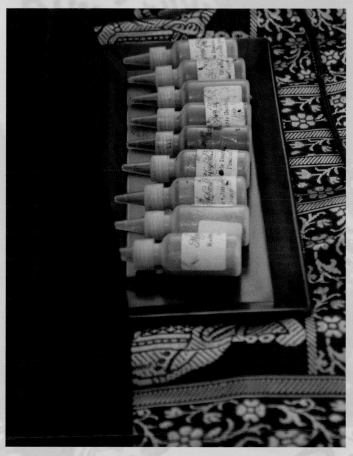

The Removal: After waiting at least four to six hours, remove the mehndi by scraping it off rather than washing it off with water. You can scrape it with the dull edge of a knife or by rubbing it off. Wash it off with water only when you have to. Don't be disappointed if the color appears orange or light brown at first. It takes hours for the color to settle, and will appear much darker the next morning. Body heat strengthens the color, that's why your palms are an ideal place to apply mehndi.

Make it Yours, This Ain't Your Grandma's Mehndi Anymore: Mehndi is now available in different colors and crystals and glitter can be incorporated in any design to match your outfit. Ask your mehndi artist about different ways to make your henna unique, or do it yourself by browsing looks online. You're literally decorating your skin, so take the time to think about how and where you want it to appear. Don't forget to add a unique design to your back shoulder, or around your belly if either will be showing during your events.

Photo by Milton Yin
Purvi gets a helping hand while the mehndi sets on her hands.

109

Your Reception

Here it is. This is the climax of your big wedding weekend. This is your moment to finally exhale, to walk into your party hand-in-hand with your husband. Bring out your bling, and get ready to dance the night away to your favorite beats.

Photo by CB Art Photography / Chandrakant Patel
Neil and Shilpi's wedding coordinated by Elegant Affairs, Virginia

Photos by Glen Barnett

Photo by CB Art Photography / Chandrakant Patel

Photos by Paul Barnett

Photo by Dallan Photography

Photo by Robert Isacson
Maria and Kavi's wedding, coordinated
by Elegant Affairs, Virginia

Photo by Paul Barnett

Photo courtesy Ateet and Jenny Ahuja
Blending two cultures, Ateet and Jenny add Latin flair by incorporating a salsa routine into their first dance.

Photo by Robert Isacson
Maria and Kavi's wedding, coordinated
by Elegant Affairs, Virginia

Words of Wisdom

My favorite part of my wedding was…

"… the wedding reception. It was the first time my husband and I could celebrate together and really let loose!"

–Eena Sidhu, June 27, 2009, Waldorf, MD

"… the way he looked at me when he saw me for the first time. And being able to share the biggest day of our lives with our close friends and family. The reception was a lot of fun too!"

–Chinar Desai, August 22, 2009, Springfield, PA

"… the reception, where we finally got to relax, dance, and have fun with all our family and guests."

–Bincy Puthenmadathi, August 11, 2007, Randolph, NJ

"… twirling in my bridal lengha as we danced our favorite salsa for the first dance."

–Jenny Ahuja, Sikh ceremony and reception, November 26, 2006, Baltimore, MD, and Catholic wedding and reception, December 2, 2006, Miami, FL

"…finally walking down the aisle and seeing my husband waiting for me. Being together for so long and growing closer together over the years had arrived to that day and moment. It was what made it so real for me."

–Poonam Rakkar, April 11, 2009, Modesto, CA

"… when my husband and I entered our reception. Everything was so beautiful, everyone was beautiful and at that point, I could relax and party."

–Meghana Acharya, June 6, 2009, San Ramon, CA

"… being carried on people's shoulders and dancing! And also, when my husband tied the 'mangalsutar' around my neck."

–Rupa Gill, May 16, 2004, Charleston, WV

"... walking out of the Fremont Sikh Temple, with my husband by my side, as Mrs. Simi Grewal-Singh."

–Simi Grewal-Singh, February 10, 2007, Fremont, CA

"... the fun I had with my family and friends whom came from near and far to celebrate with us on one of the most joyous days of my life. It was a true blessing to get married and have my loved ones surrounding me, witnessing and celebrating, my marriage."

–Nazia Khan, July 18, 2008, Chicago, IL

"... when my mamas brought me to the mandap in a doli. I felt like a princess who was finally going to be with her prince forever—it was the best moment of the wedding by far!"

–Kajal Patel, June 27, 2009, Cherry Hill, NJ

"... marrying my best friend."

–Ameeta Singh, June 3, 2006, Fairfax, VA

"... during the beginning of the wedding ceremony when we saw each other for the first time and exchanged smiles. We both knew in that moment that we were meant for each other."

–Navleen Sandhu, October 29, 2005, Gaithersburg, MD

"... the reception, everything about it was amazing and it was the best night of our lives!"

–Tanisha Gulhar, May 24, 2008, Reston Town Center, VA

Section IV: Wedding Diaries from Real Weddings

"The minute I heard my first love story
I started looking for you,
not knowing how blind that was.
Lovers don't finally meet somewhere.
They're in each other all along."

—Rumi

Photos courtesy Aparna and Sunil

Aparna and Sunil

When Aparna, a Tamil Brahmin and Sunil, a Keralite Catholic decided to get married, they faced initial resistance from their parents. There are just too many differences, the parents said.

But after years of dating, Aparna and Sunil knew they wanted to marry. With much thought and guidance from their religious officiates, the couple planned a unique, inter-faith ceremony that honored both cultures and religions with equal respect. Though planning was tedious, the process exposed Aparna and Sunil to each other's heritage.

"We wanted to bring our religions and families together, to integrate, and show how similar we actually are, and how we believe in the same values and commitments," said Aparna.

The 300-person wedding took place on Memorial Day weekend in Washington, DC's dramatic Melon Auditorium. The wedding was an intricately choreographed ceremony, a back-and-forth between Hindu and Catholic rites, with Tamil, Malayalee, and American elements fused along the way. Within the hour and a half ceremony, the couple exchanged garlands and vows, listened to a Ganesh Puja, listened to readings from the Bible, and honored the light of both the sacred fire and unity candle.

"It really was such a unique ceremony. It was so personal," she said. "By the end of it, we were just so happy to be married, and so ready to celebrate."

The reception that followed was no less personal, with speeches from both fathers, dances staged by close friends, and a special song composed and performed by Sunil's brother.

Tips from a real bride:

"Decide what's important to you, what you and your family really care about. Set your priorities and spend your time, energy and money towards those goals."

"Insist on reading and signing a contract with each vendor. Among South Asians, vendors tend to be more informal…they'll give you their word instead of a formal contract."

125

Neha and Nipun

For Neha, through a modern day, semi-arranged marriage she found her soul mate.

Some love stories need a matchmaker to get things started. In Neha's case, that match-maker was her cousin Sarina.

"So, there's this guy," Sarina said one day. She described her co-worker Nipun and asked Neha if she'd be interested in talking to him. Thinking nothing of it, Neha casually agreed. Later that day she received an e-mail from Nipun, and after a few e-mail exchanges and a phone call, they decided to meet that Sunday. Their chemistry was immediate and undeni-able. After another few rapid-fire days of talking and family introductions, the couple agreed that they were a good fit, a perfect match as future life partners. *Five days after meeting each other, they were engaged. "We're soul mates,"* said Neha.

Scheduling conflicts forced the couple to rush and plan a wedding that summer, but again fate helped them along the way—as they inquired for venues during peak wedding season, a Saturday date unexpectedly became available at a popular Virginia wedding venue called Foxchase Manor. Could it be a sign?

Guests flew in from around the world and across the country to celebrate Neha and Nipun's union.

Photos by Ayesha Khwaja Husain

Tips from a real bride:

"Though I don't recommend it, trust me when I say that a wedding can come together in a short time."

Shveta and Arjun

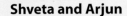

"We knew we wanted to face the water..."

For Shveta and Arjun, it was a traditional Hindu wedding with tropical island flare.

While on vacation in Bermuda, they slipped away to a quiet spot on the island. As the sun set into the crystal blue waters around them, Arjun proposed to Shveta.

The next day the newly engaged pair sat in the hotel restaurant, suddenly aware of the wedding planning responsibilities ahead.

"The thought of planning a big wedding wasn't very appealing," said Shveta.

From Virginia to Calcutta, the couple has family all around the world, and logistics for a wedding seemed overwhelming at first. As they brainstormed ideas, they noticed a wedding party filing into the hotel lobby. Suddenly, an idea:

"Why don't we get married here in Bermuda?!" said Shveta.

What started off as instant inspiration evolved into a picture perfect wedding weekend in Bermuda one year later.

The couple's choice of a destination wedding didn't prompt much protest from their families, though Shveta and Arjun worked to respect both parents' wish lists. Each set of parents hosted wedding parties in their respective cities, but the heart of the celebration was in Bermuda.

More than 30 friends and family joined the couple for a weekend of festivities that kicked off with a beach barbecue the night before the ceremony. Tiki torches and Rajasthani table clothes set the mood for an island party and an Indian buffet was set up beachside. Indian tunes blasted from their boombox and aunties sang and played on a dholki, giving the night a *tropical* sangeet vibe. Dressed in a "beachy sundress," Shveta literally danced the night away with Arjun and her guests.

The next day the couple completed pre-wedding rituals, like the choora ceremony and applying haldi to the skin, at the hotel with their respective parents. Then the traditional Hindu wedding ceremony, officiated by a pandit that the couple had flown in, began. Shveta wore a traditional silk sari and her mother's wedding jewelry. Deep pink flowers and greenery hung from the mandap and guests used palm-sized leaves to fan themselves on that hot day. The mandap was set against a breathtaking, natural backdrop.

"We knew we wanted to face the water," said Shveta. "We had found a perfect plateau that overlooked the ocean—it was just gorgeous."

Photos courtesty Shveta Berry

130

"When you get married in such a beautiful location, you don't have to spend a lot on decorations," she said.

Evening rain showers forced the reception indoors, but the event didn't lose any island charm. *Dark and Stormy*, a Bermudian specialty, was the cocktail of the night, and the dinner menu was infused with local flavors like fish chowder.

Looking back on her destination wedding weekend, Shveta wouldn't change a thing.

"The best part was that I actually got to spend time with every single guest. The day after the wedding, we all lounged at the pool together," she said. "It was like the party just kept going."

Tips from a real bride:

"When you have a destination wedding, don't worry about the small stuff. Worry about having good food and drinks, because everyone is already enjoying being on vacation."

"Don't be afraid to ask for what you want. If a hotel doesn't offer something, tell them exactly what you need… usually they can make it happen. Our hotel had never done an Indian wedding before."

131

Anoopa and Kabir

Some love stories start early in life.

Kabir and Anoopa have known each other almost since they were born. There's a photo of the two as children, only about five years old, at a birthday party waiting patiently side by side at the end of a table for their share of cake. Their parents had become friends in the early '70s when they had first moved to America, years before Anoopa and Kabir were born. The families shared milestones like birthdays and Diwalis, and were truly family-friends.

But things changed in 1984. Silently divided by the violence and politics back in India at the time, an unspoken tension seared through their local Indian community. Hindu families and Sikh families subtly parted ways for a brief time. Though the community and their families proved resilient and reconciled soon after, it would be years before Anoopa from a Hindu background and Kabir from a Sikh background connected on a personal level.

"I went to her sweet sixteen party," Kabir said. "But we hardly said a word to each other. At the time, we knew *of* each other, but we didn't really know each other," he said.

A few more casual run-ins at family parties and local cultural events and the two developed a lasting bond.

"I remember telling my friend when I was only 17, that I could see myself getting married to Kabir," she said.

Years later when Kabir and Anoopa married, their wedding respected both Sikh and Hindu faiths, and truly celebrated the vibrant local community that was such an integral backdrop in their families' lives. They wanted their reception to have an intimate feel, and with a heartfelt, personal welcome from the bride and groom, and a one-of-a-kind serenade for the bride by Kabir, theirs was a reception to remember.

Photos by Glenn Barnett

132

Years later when Kabir and Anoopa married, their wedding respected both Sikh and Hindu faiths, and truly celebrated the vibrant local community that was such an integral backdrop in their families' lives.

Tonushree and Kush
Love Letters

If you ever doubted that fate guides the heart, you haven't heard Tonushree and Kush's love story. I'll share their story through Tonushree's own words. On their wedding website, she wrote:

As old fashioned as it sounds, Kush and I fell in love through our letters. Long, handwritten letters that we exchanged for nearly six months before we ever spoke a word on the phone or even saw a photo of each other. We were introduced through eHarmony, after I filled out their personality profile on a whim one October night. I never actually signed up for their matching service, but the next day, without warning, seven "matches" appeared in my inbox. Kush was the very first one.

I was enchanted by his profile, so I did what any self-respecting researcher would do: I googled him, and luckily, discovered his blog. There I found an amazing collection of photographs, personal reflections on politics and poetry and family and life, and generally speaking, the rough sketch of a person I thought I might want to know better. But when I clicked on the "contact me" link, instead of an e-mail address or phone number, I found his mailing address, along with this note:

If for some reason you want to contact me and you don't have my information, send me a letter. I love getting letters, and I promise I'll write back.

So I took a deep breath, and did just that. I bought some pretty paper, and began by introducing myself as the girl from eHarmony, sharing some funny stories (like how I had burned my blinds during a Diwali party I threw that weekend), and asking if he maybe wanted to be pen pals? Two weeks later, true to his word, he wrote back. And for the next several months, we got to know each other in this way—through our words and the shape of our handwriting and the stories of our lives. And at some point, without knowing it or understanding it, we began to fall in love. After the 7th letter, I flew to Santa Fe, got off the plane and ran into his arms.

That's how our story began.

Photo by Melissa Keeley for Telltale Photography
Tonushree and Kush's wedding

138

Photos by Melissa Keeley for Telltale Photography
Getting ready

Melissa Keeley for Telltale Photography
Walking around the sacred fire

*Melissa Keeley for
Telltale Photography*
Kush waits behind
the pink cloth

Nicole Haley for Telltale Photography

Tips from a real bride:

"Trust your instincts when you're wedding planning, and don't rush it. You know what's best for you."

Words of Wisdom

The three words that best describe my wedding are…

"Fun, memorable, and family-oriented."

–Eena Sidhu, June 27, 2009, Waldorf, MD

"Elegant, colorful, FUN!"

–Chinar Desai, August 22, 2009, Springfield, PA

"Memorable, enjoyable, beautiful."

–Bincy Puthenmadathi, August 11, 2007, Randolph, NJ

"International love fest."

–Jenny Ahuja, Sikh ceremony and reception, November 26, 2006, Baltimore, MD, and Catholic wedding and reception, December 2, 2006, Miami, FL

"Unforgettable. Exciting. Gorgeous."

–Poonam Rakkar, April 11, 2009, Modesto, CA

"Colorful; entertaining; love."

–Meghana Acharya, June 6, 2009, San Ramon, CA

"Vibrant, elegant, memorable."

–Rupa Gill, May 16, 2004, Charleston, WV

"Memorable, festive, and colorful."

–Simi Grewal-Singh, February 10, 2007, Fremont, CA

"East meets west."

–Nazia Khan, July 18, 2008, Chicago, IL

"Fun, memorable, romantic, or Ready, Set, Go!"

–Kajal Patel, June 27, 2009, Cherry Hill, New Jersey

"Colorful, spiritual, and fun!!"

–Ameeta Singh, June 3, 2006, Fairfax, VA

"Elegant, whimsical, and loving."

–Navleen Sandhu, October 29, 2005, Gaithersburg, MD

"Fun, happy, perfect."

–Tanisha Gulhar, May 24, 2008, Reston Town Center, VA

Resources

Featured Vendors

A special thank you to the following for sharing with me their time and expertise:

Photography

AISM Photography
www.aismphotography.com

CB ART Photography / Chandrakant Patel
http://cbartphotography.com

Paul Barnett Photography
www.paulbarnettphotography.com

Dallan Photography
www.dallanphotography.com

Robert Isacson
www.isacsonstudios.com

Yogi Patel of Global Photography LA
www.globalphotography.net

Telltale Photography
www.telltalephotography.com

Milton Yin
www.miltonyin.com

Planning

Engaging Affairs
www.engagingaffairs.com

Hair/Makeup/Mehndi

Suman Khosla
http://sumankhosla.com

Ziba Beauty Salons
www.zibabeauty.com

Clothing

Prabhleen Bindra, Gurdiya Couture
www.gurdiyacouture.com

Priti Malhotra, Illusions Designs
www.illusions-designs.com

Stationary

Saima Says Designs
www.saimasaysdesign.com

Wedding Customs from Around India

Punjab: Sikh or Hindu

Thaka or Roka: Agreement between the bride and groom and their families.

Mangni, Sagaai or Kudmai: Engagement and ring exchange.

Shri Akhand Path (Sikh): Uninterrupted reading of the holy Guru Granth Sahib from beginning to end.

Chunni Chadana: Female relatives from the groom's family bring gifts of clothes, jewelry, henna, fruits, dried fruits, and more for the bride and drape her head with a "chunni" or head scarf, usually in a festive color of red.

Sangeet: Festive, pre-wedding celebration with song and dance.

Mehndi: The bride's henna ceremony.

Kangna Bandhana (Hindu): Tying of the sacred "mouli" thread on both the bride and groom in their respective houses. The couple will later try to untie the knots in each other's bracelets.

Uptan or Vatna: The haldi ceremony. Uptan is a paste made from sandalwood, turmeric, and rose water that is applied by married female members of the families to the faces, hands, and feet of the bride and groom in their respective homes.

Choora Chadana (bride): The bride's maternal uncle gifts her with ivory and red colored bangles, a sign of a newlywed. Also at this time, unmarried girls of "marriageable" age tie *kaleeras,* or dangling ornaments, on the bride's choora.

Sehrabandhi (groom): Tying of the traditional headdress on the groom.

Ghodi Sajana: Traditionally, the groom arrives to the wedding on a white mare. The groom's sister and female relatives decorate and feed the horse, *ghodi*, that will carry the groom in the baraat.

Baraat: Groom's wedding procession to the marriage ceremony.

Milni: Welcoming the groom and introducing the two families.

Aarti (Hindu): The bride's mother performs the *aarti*, a traditional Hindu welcome ritual with a lamp, or *diya*, placed on a platter, or *thali*, to welcome her son-in-law-to-be.

Anand Karaj or Lavan Phera (Sikh): The Sikh wedding ceremony (see page 62 for more).

Shaadi (Hindu): The Hindu wedding ceremony (see page 52 for more).

Doli: Sending off the bride.

Reception: Post wedding celebrations

Gujarat: Hindu[1]

Chandlo: Agreement by the bride, groom, and families. A priest blesses the couple and applies a red vermillion dot, or *chandlo*, to their foreheads. The couple exchanges garlands and the families give gifts to the bride and groom.

Ganesh Sthapan /Ganesh Matli: This first *puja*, or prayer ceremony, honors Lord Ganesha and is the first of all the wedding events. It is an intimate event held in both the bride and groom's homes.

Mehendi: Henna ceremony

Garba: A festive night of song and dance, where guests dance traditional Gujarati dances, garba and dandia.

Pithi: The pithi ceremony takes place in both bride and groom's homes. A paste called pithi is made of sandalwood powder, turmeric, oils, and rose water is applied on the faces, arms, and legs of the bride and groom by members of their family.

Mandva Mahurat: Puja to Lord Ganesh to bless the area where the wedding ceremony will take place.

Griha Shanti: A religious ceremony conducted to seek the blessing and harmony between the two families.

Mameru Mosaalu: The bride receives gifts of jewelry, bangles, and saris from her maternal uncle.

Baraat: The groom's wedding procession to the marriage ceremony.

Var Ponke: The bride's mother welcomes the groom by performing aarti at the entrance of the wedding venue.

Lagna: The wedding ceremony begins (see page 52 for more).

Bengal: Hindu[2]

The Ashirbaad: Agreement between the bride, groom, and families. A wedding date is decided on. The elders bless the couple by showering them with *dhaan* (husked rice) and *dooba* (three bladed grass).

Aai Buddo Bhaat: The bride's last meal as a maiden in her parents' home. A joyful, mini-feast, this meal is often shared with family and friends.

Gai Halood: Close female relatives apply a tumeric paste on the bride.

Shaka Paula: Seven married ladies adorn the bride with coral and shell bangles. They feed her *Dahi Mangal* (yogurt and rice), after which she fasts until the marriage ceremony is over.

Boijotri: The wedding procession. With the blowing of the conch, the wedding procession sets off for the ceremony.

Potto Bastra: Welcoming the groom. The bride's family receives the groom and presents him with sweets and gifts.

The Wedding: Actual wedding rites are divided into the following segments:

Saat Paak: The bride's face is hidden with betel leaves. Sitting on a low wooden stool, called *pidi*, she is lifted by her brothers and taken around the groom in seven complete circles.

Shubh Dhristi: The betel leaves on the bride are moved apart to enable the couple to make eye contact for the shubh dhristi, or viewing, in front of their guests.

The couple then exchanges garlands and the groom proceeds to the mandap (marriage platform) followed by the bride (see page 52 for more).

Tamil[3]

Panda Kaal: A puja sometimes to the Lord Ganesh sets the tone for a peaceful wedding.

Nalangu: The day before the wedding, the groom and his family are welcomed by the bride's family and given flowers, fruits and sweets.

Vratham & Pallikai Thellichal: Both bride and groom's families fast the day before the wedding. In the Pallikai Thellichal ritual, clay pots are filled with grains and left to soak while traditional folk songs are sung.

Naandi: A ceremony honoring a family's ancestors.

Nicchiyadhartham: The groom's family gives the bride a sari. She is also given sweets, flowers, and fruits and is blessed by aarti.

Lagna Pathirigai: The priest announces the details of the wedding.

Mangala snaanam: The bride and groom bathe in their respective homes on the day of the wedding

Oonjal: Exchange of garlands. The bride and groom are then seated to begin the wedding ceremony. Read more about the actual wedding rituals on page 52.

1 http://weddings.iloveindia.com/gujarati-wedding/pre-wedding-rituals.html

   http://wedding.dharmeshpatel.com/marriage_ceremony/var_ponke

2 www.marriagemantra.com/bengali_community.html

   http://weddings.iloveindia.com/bengali-wedding/index.html

3 http://weddings.iloveindia.com/tamil-wedding/index.html

   www.come2india.org/tamil-wedding.html